What Were
the Salem Witch Trials?

What Were the Salem Witch Trials?

by Joan Holub

illustrated by Dede Putra

Grosset & Dunlap
An Imprint of Penguin Random House

GROSSET & DUNLAP
Penguin Young Readers Group
An Imprint of Penguin Random House LLC

Text copyright © 2015 by Joan Holub. Illustrations copyright © 2015 by Penguin Random House LLC. All rights reserved. Published by Grosset & Dunlap, an imprint of Penguin Random House LLC, 345 Hudson Street, New York, New York 10014. GROSSET & DUNLAP is a trademark of Penguin Random House LLC. Printed in the USA.

Library of Congress Cataloging-in-Publication Data is available.

ISBN 978-0-448-47905-7   10 9 8 7 6 5 4 3 2 1

Contents

What Were the Salem Witch Trials?

In the winter of 1692, trouble came to the village of Salem in the Massachusetts Bay Colony. Witch trouble!

Suddenly, two girls got a strange illness. Their bodies twitched and shuddered. They spoke nonsense and seemed to be choking. They said they were being pinched and poked by something invisible. Soon more girls in Salem began acting strangely, too. If this was an illness, no one could find a cure.

Some villagers thought it might be the work of witches! Witches were serious stuff in the New England colonies. Scary stuff. Many people believed witches were real and that they wanted to hurt people. A hunt began in Salem to catch and punish the witches who were making the girls sick. But who were the witches? Could they be neighbors? Family members? Frightened villagers panicked. They pointed fingers at one another and cried, "Witch!"

Over the next ten months, about two hundred people in Salem Village and surrounding areas were accused of witchcraft. Most were women. A few were children. Almost all went to jail. There were trials. There were hangings. Innocent people were convicted of witchcraft and killed. It was horrible! For a while, it seemed there would be no end to this awful time. But eventually, the witch hunt did stop and so did the trials.

So, what was really going on in Salem in 1692?

CHAPTER 1
Betty and Abigail

It was a freezing cold day in January 1692 when nine-year-old Betty Parris first started acting weird. Really weird. She hid under chairs. She flapped her arms and jerked around. She babbled wildly, saying words no one could understand. Other times, she screamed or couldn't speak at all.

Betty and her family lived in Salem Village. It was a farming community of about 525 people in the Massachusetts Bay Colony, next to Salem Town.

Puritans

Puritan is the name given to a certain kind of Christian in the early 1600s. Originally Puritans lived in England. But they didn't want to belong to the Church of England. They didn't believe in fancy churches with stained-glass windows and golden statues. In their church, they sat on hard wooden benches. They believed the words in the Bible were the law. Many Puritans left England for America in hope of practicing religion their own way. In 1692, most of the settlers in the Massachusetts Bay Colony, including Salem, were Puritans. As for Puritan children, they were expected to work hard and obey their parents, especially their fathers. Their parents loved them. However, part of Puritan parents' responsibility was to cure their children of stubbornness and pride. Puritans believed that discipline would keep children close to God and far from the Devil. That way, the Devil couldn't trick them into doing his evil work.

The Parrises belonged to the Puritan church. In fact, Betty's father was the Salem Village minister. Her parents were very worried about her. What was this strange illness? Not knowing what else to call it, they said she was having "fits."

Whatever was wrong with her, it was catching. Her cousin, eleven-year-old Abigail Williams, started acting the same way. Abigail was an orphan. She lived with the Parris family after her own parents died.

Betty and Abigail had been good, quiet girls. But now they screeched and shivered. They felt dull pains and acted scared. This went on for weeks.

Neither girl had a rash or a fever, so they didn't have smallpox, measles, or malaria. These were the diseases that New England colonists often died from. And why didn't Betty's brother, sister, or parents catch the sickness, too? Why didn't the family's slaves, Tituba and her husband, John Indian, get sick?

Betty's parents tried simple home remedies. Maybe a dose of parsnip seeds would work, or castor oil mixed with amber. They prayed for the girls to get well. The neighbors prayed for them, too. Nothing helped.

In late February, a doctor named William
Griggs came to examine the girls. He did not think
they were sick. He thought they were "under an
evil hand." In other words, they were bewitched!

In 1692, this was not a strange thing for a
doctor to think.

The day after the doctor came, Mr. and Mrs.
Parris went to a meeting. They left the children
home with Tituba. It was a Thursday, and

Thursdays in New England were lecture days. Colonists would gather at meetinghouses or churches. Reverend Parris planned to alert people that witches might be among them in Salem Village. He would ask other ministers to come try to help Betty and Abigail.

While Betty's parents were gone, a neighbor named Mary Sibley came to the Parris house.

She gave Tituba and John a recipe. A recipe for something called a witch cake. It was like a big biscuit. It was supposed to be a cure for witchcraft. At least that's what they hoped.

The recipe was disgusting. It went like this: Mix rye flour with some of the girls' urine to make a sort of dough. Then pat the dough into a cake shape, bake it in the hot ashes of the fireplace, and feed it to a dog.

While the dog ate the cake, the witch was supposed to feel every bite of its teeth. She would come to the house and beg for the pain to stop. That way the witch could be caught. Some people even thought a dog who had eaten a witch cake might bark out the witch's name!

Tituba and John Indian made a witch cake. They were trying to help. They hoped the cake would show who was causing the strange sickness in Betty and Abigail. But, of course, it didn't.

The witch cake had not worked. So, now what?

Massachusetts Bay Colony

In 1630, about one thousand Puritan colonists in eleven ships sailed west from England across the Atlantic Ocean. They settled the Massachusetts Bay Colony. There was already a small farming village on the coast named Salem. Over the next ten years, more than twenty thousand Puritans would move to the Massachusetts Bay Colony. Boston became the capital in 1632. Salem Village remained a poor farming community. Merchants and richer people settled in nearby Salem Town, which was a busy seaport. Salem Village is now called Danvers. Salem Town became the city of Salem.

Massachusetts Bay Colony

Salem Village
Salem
Boston
Plymouth

14

CHAPTER 2
Witches

Betty's parents were angry when they found out about the cake. Witch cakes were folk magic. The Puritan church was against the use of such magic. Ministers like Betty's father thought practicing folk magic was a sin. They feared it could open the door to spirits and let evil enter the real world.

After the witch cake, Betty and Abigail only got worse. They gasped for air as if they were being choked. Their bodies bent and twisted like they were puppets being jerked on strings. They claimed to see things no one else could see— ghostly figures, which were pinching, biting, and hitting them. That's why they'd been jumping around and twitching.

Superstitions

Many people in Salem believed in magic, both good and bad. They were very afraid of bad magic, and thought witches and demons were to blame for it. They believed that witches and demons enjoyed causing sadness and trouble. Like the sudden death of a baby or a sick cow. A house burning down. Crops dying. Puritans tried hard to attract good luck. They might nail a horseshoe by the door. They'd spread bay leaves around the outside of their houses.

Some people carried a piece of mountain ash—its nickname was witchwood—in their pockets to keep witches away.

Many New Englanders believed that witches had spirits inside them that they controlled. These spirits were called specters. They were invisible to most people and could fly. A witch could send her specter long distances to harm others. A specter was said to look like the witch who sent it.

Mr. Parris, other ministers, and neighbors kept asking the girls questions. Could they see the faces of the witches who were hurting them? What were their names? The grown-ups said Betty and Abigail had to tell them! It was the only way the witches could be stopped, and then the girls would get well.

By now, the two girls knew that the grown-ups thought invisible witch specters were tormenting them. It was a scary idea! Betty and Abigail probably feared it was true.

Maybe they got so scared that they panicked. Who could the witches be? The girls must have thought hard in hopes of figuring it out. Perhaps

the grown-ups even suggested suspects to them.
Finally the girls came up with a name. Tituba!
She was the witch.

Although Tituba was in another room, Betty
and Abigail shouted in terror. They said her
specter had whooshed over to hurt them, and that
she pinched them and poked them with pins.
They could see her specter moving around even
though no one else could. At least, that's the story
the two girls told.

Tituba had taken care of Betty as well as her older brother and younger sister for many years. Why would she suddenly act so mean? No one asked her. They just figured the Devil had made her do it.

The girls named two more witches—Sarah Good and Sarah Osborne. Women didn't have much power back then. They couldn't vote. They couldn't own property unless they inherited it, and even then, they had to get the government's permission to sell it. Men were the bosses. Women were accused of witchcraft far more often than men. Not many people liked Sarah Good and Sarah Osborne, so the girls probably knew no one would stand up for them. And Tituba was a slave. Slaves didn't count for much, either.

Soon, two other girls in Salem Village reported witch trouble. It seemed that a witch's specter was now pinching a twelve-year-old girl named Ann Putnam.

Ann claimed that the witch was Sarah Good, the same woman that Betty and Abigail had named! After that, seventeen-year-old Elizabeth Hubbard, a friend of Betty and Abigail's, chimed in. She announced that Sarah Good had magically sent a wolf to chase her.

Now it seemed there were four victims of witchcraft. Whom would the witches strike next? The villagers were sure about one thing. Something had to be done to stop them.

On February 29, Ann Putnam's father and three other men went for help. It was a terrible day to travel. It was storming with wild winds and flooded roads. Salem Town was about five miles away from the village and was big enough to have judges. There, the four men filed a complaint.

They charged Tituba, Sarah Good, and Sarah Osborne with "suspicion of witchcraft."

By the next morning, Salem Town officials had picked up all three women. There was no courthouse, so they were taken to a tavern in Salem Village. Right away, the tavern keeper's wife checked to see if they had any unusual moles, warts, or birthmarks. Having a strange mark on your skin was considered a sign you were a witch. Witches supposedly communicated with certain kinds of spirits, called familiars, through these marks. Familiars, which often appeared as animals, helped witches do their dirty, evil work.

Tituba, Sarah Good, and Sarah Osborne didn't have such marks. They'd passed the test. Still, it didn't mean they weren't witches as far as the Puritans were concerned. The three women would still be questioned.

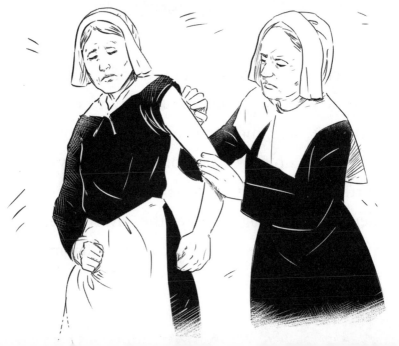

CHAPTER 3
Questions

The news traveled fast. It was still winter, so people were not yet busy planting crops. They had time on their hands. A big crowd gathered, eager to see what would happen to the suspects. The idea that witches were making trouble in Salem was scary, but fascinating.

Soon the tavern was overflowing. Everyone moved to the meetinghouse, which was also

Old Salem Meetinghouse

the church. Local judges John Hathorne and Jonathan Corwin were in charge. The four girls, Betty, Abigail, Ann, and Elizabeth, were there.

One at a time, the three suspects were brought in. This wasn't a trial. The judges were just supposed to ask questions. Then they would decide if this was all nonsense or not. If they suspected something troubling, the women would later be questioned again in a real trial.

Sarah Good went first. She was very poor. So poor that she dressed in rags. She often went around begging for food with her baby and her four-year-old daughter, Dorcas. Earlier that winter, she had begged at Betty's house. Mr. Parris remembered giving food to Dorcas, but Sarah didn't seem grateful. When she left his house, she was muttering grumpily to herself. Now Mr. Parris wondered if she might have been saying a spell or curse—one that bewitched Betty and Abigail!

The two judges questioned Sarah Good. But they didn't ask *if* she was hurting the girls. They asked her *why* she was hurting them. They had already decided she was guilty. All they wanted was her confession. If they got her to say she was a witch, they wouldn't need witnesses or proof.

However, Sarah Good insisted that she wasn't hurting the children. She said she wasn't a witch. She said that she had only been mumbling her thanks to Mr. Parris for the food that day.

A man named Ezekiel Cheever wrote everything down. He wrote the questions and the answers given. He also made notes about how Betty, Abigail, Ann, Elizabeth, and the witch suspects acted. But what he wrote wasn't very fair. He said that Sarah Good told lies and acted wickedly. That was only his opinion, not fact.

Sarah Osborne went next. She was sick. It was hard for her to walk, so she hadn't gone to church in a year. Puritans didn't accept that as a

Ezekiel Cheever

good reason. People were supposed to try hard to attend church, no matter what. Betty and Abigail said Sarah Osborne had magically visited them in the shape of a bird. A bird with Sarah's head! Black cats are usually associated with witches on Halloween today. But in Salem, the girls said they often saw witches with birds.

Sarah Osborne spoke up to defend herself. Right away, the four girls began to shudder, screech, and fall to the floor. Even though Sarah Osborne hadn't moved, they said she was attacking them. Or rather, her specter was. But only the girls could see it.

After lunch, it was Tituba's turn to be questioned. The girl accusers shrieked and howled when she was brought in. They squirmed and twisted like they were in pain. She would have her work cut out for her to make everyone believe she was innocent.

Tituba and John

In his twenties, Mr. Parris lived in Barbados, where he probably bought Tituba to be his slave. Barbados is an island in the Caribbean Sea, northeast of South America. Tituba and her husband, John, may have originally been Arawak Indians taken from South America and forced into slavery on Barbados. English Puritans feared Native Americans, whom they called "Indians." An Indian like Tituba probably seemed suspicious and strange to them as well.

CHAPTER 4
Tituba

At first, Tituba told the judges she was not a witch. She insisted she wasn't hurting the girls. But the judges kept asking questions, on and on.

Surprise! Eventually she confessed. She said she really was a witch. People in the crowd gasped. A real witch lived in the village minister's home? This proved that the Devil could strike anywhere.

Tituba went on to say, "The Devil came to me and bid me serve him." The judges asked what he looked like. She replied that he was a man who offered her gifts including a yellow bird, and that he'd told her to sign his book.

This is how Puritans thought you became a witch. First the Devil came and asked you to become his servant. He made you sign his special book, using your blood as ink. Working for the Devil meant harming people. In return, he gave you magic powers and didn't hurt you. If you didn't want to join the Devil, he would probably keep bugging you. You had to be strong to fight him.

What did Tituba tell the Devil? the judges wanted to know. At first, she'd said no way! She wasn't going to work for him. But he said he would kill her if she didn't sign. He would never let Betty and Abigail get well and might even kill them, too. She didn't want that. So she signed

the Devil's book with her blood. She claimed that she'd also seen other names in the book, nine besides her own. Sarah Good's name was in the book. Also Sarah Osborne's. In other words, she was saying that they were witches, too.

Tituba went on to say that all three of their specters had ridden together on a stick to Ann Putnam's house. The other two women had tried to make her use a knife to kill Ann. To make matters worse, Ann agreed this visit had happened.

The crowd was very scared. If everything Tituba had revealed was true, there must be seven more witches on the loose.

Tituba's confession had stunned everyone that day. But it was exactly what the two judges wanted to hear. It meant there would be trials so they could expose evil witches and punish them. Tituba, Sarah Good, and Sarah Osborne went to jail. That very night, some men claimed they saw a terrible creature leap into the sky. It turned into the three women's specters. Then it disappeared!

CHAPTER 5
Witch Hunt

Soon, still more Salem girls talked of being attacked by an invisible evil force. Something was pricking them with pins, pinching them, and hurting them.

What made them say this? Perhaps seeing what had happened to Betty, Abigail, Ann, and Elizabeth made these other girls grow scared. If they felt an odd pain, perhaps they wondered if an invisible witch had caused it. Or did these girls just want the same attention that Betty, Abigail, Ann, and Elizabeth were getting?

At first, the girls in Salem targeted poor people, troublemakers, and oddballs. That's who they said were witches. It might start with a girl recalling something strange you once said. A person would tell someone else and maybe make it sound a little weirder than it had been. Why? Maybe the person didn't like you. Or was jealous of you.

Anyone who was different seemed suspect. Women who argued or were stubborn or flirty or pushy. People who had too many or not enough children.

People who were very rich or very poor. People who didn't go to church. Or who broke Puritan rules like not riding your horse on Sundays. If butter or milk happened to spoil when you were around, you could be called a witch.

So far, all the people accused of witchcraft were grown women. Then on March 3, Ann Putnam said that Sarah Good's four-year-old daughter, Dorcas, was a witch. She claimed that Dorcas's specter had choked her.

Dorcas Good

Three days later, Ann Putnam said that the specter of a woman named Elizabeth Proctor had choked, bitten, and pinched her. So Elizabeth Proctor was added to the list of witch suspects. Her

John and Elizabeth Proctor

maid, Mary Warren, had recently begun having fits like the other girls. Mrs. Proctor's husband, John, thought Mary and all the others were faking it. John was a hotheaded man. He said what he thought, and he demanded that Mary stop all the nonsense. But in return, Mary said that she was being attacked by *his* specter now, too. The list of witch suspects kept growing.

Soon Mary Warren and Ann Putnam also accused Martha Corey, a good churchgoer, of attacking them. Ann said Martha's specter tried to make her bite off her own tongue! Ann Putnam was part of the small group of girl ringleaders who would continue naming witches throughout the trials. However, there would be many other accusers, ranging from age four to over eighty years old!

Ann's cousin, seventeen-year-old Mary Walcott, soon joined the accusers. Sometimes in the courtroom, Walcott would calmly do her knitting as the other girl accusers had wild fits around her. Other times she and the girls would show teeth marks or pins sticking in their skin where they'd supposedly been bitten or poked by a witch suspect.

Suspected witch Martha Corey was questioned later that March. Ann Putnam, Ann's mother, their servant Mercy Lewis, Abigail Williams, and Elizabeth Hubbard were there. Whenever Martha made a move, all of them made the exact same move. If Martha folded her arms, all five folded theirs. If she turned her head, they turned theirs. They claimed Martha Corey's magic was making them copy her. It was as if they were puppets forced to dance to her evil tune.

The Proctors were questioned on April 11. Plenty of people were annoyed at John because he thought the girls were faking and should be beaten for it. This made a lot of believers mad, including Mr. Parris. At Elizabeth Proctor's questioning, Ann Putnam and Abigail Williams tried to hit

her. However their fists stopped short as if some unseen force had blocked them. Was evil magic at work? The Proctors were thrown in jail.

McCarthy and Modern Witch Hunts

In the 1950s, Wisconsin senator Joseph McCarthy went on a hunt. People now sometimes call it a witch hunt. However, it was actually a hunt for people in the United States who McCarthy believed were Communists. In Communist countries, there is no democracy. There is only one political party and little freedom. In the years after World War II, many people in America were scared that Communism would take over the world. McCarthy played on this fear. He said there were Communist spies all over the country, and that they wanted to overthrow the US government. Thousands of Americans were questioned, especially those who worked in the military, labor unions, or the entertainment industry. There were FBI investigations. There was an unofficial Hollywood blacklist. It was a list of names of suspects in the entertainment industry. If you were unlucky enough to get on the list, you might lose your job. Many innocent people did, and some even went to jail. There was mass panic. By 1954, this terrible hunt was over.

Joseph McCarthy

The Crucible

A writer named Arthur Miller was questioned during the McCarthy witch hunt. However, he refused to tell the names of other writers he had talked to about Communism. Because of this, his name was put on the blacklist. He wrote a play called *The Crucible* (CROO-sih-bil). A crucible, in this case, is a test or trial. His play showed how the Salem witch hunt and McCarthyism were alike. Once you were accused of being a witch or a Communist, it was hard to prove otherwise, and it unfairly ruined your life. *The Crucible* was first performed in 1953 on Broadway in New York City. It is one of the most famous plays ever written in America.

Arthur Miller

CHAPTER 6
Trials

By April, more people were being accused of witchcraft almost every day. Soon the suspects began to notice something interesting. Because she had confessed, Tituba wasn't put in chains.

She had also asked for forgiveness for using black magic. Asking forgiveness was believed to help push the Devil away. However, Sarah Good and Sarah Osborne had not confessed. So they were chained to the wall in jail.

Obviously, people who confessed got better treatment. Some suspects' families begged them to confess. It seemed the smart thing to do. In the Massachusetts Bay Colony, the punishment for witchcraft was death. Fear led about forty suspects to lie and tell the judges they, too, were witches. Unfortunately, this made it seem as if the girls who'd accused them must be telling the truth!

When Tituba confessed, she gave the names of other witches. This had helped her as well. Other witch suspects noticed this. So not only did they confess, they gave names of other supposed witches, too.

Seventeen-year-old Margaret Jacobs was accused of witchcraft by Abigail Williams. First Margaret Jacobs lied and confessed that she was a witch. When that wasn't enough to satisfy the judges, she named other witches, including the former Salem minister George Burroughs, and even her grandfather! (Later she said it wasn't true and that she was very sorry to have done that.)

Even little four-year-old Dorcas supplied the name of a witch suspect. Her own mother, Sarah Good.

By May, the jails were getting full. Jails were dirty and cold. There were rats, lice, and mold. There might be one bucket for all the prisoners to use for a toilet. Germs quickly passed from one person to another. People got sick living like this.

In jail, you had to pay for your food and water. You had to pay for clean straw to sleep on. And you had to pay for the chains around your ankles or wrists. If you couldn't pay your fees, you'd never get out of jail, even if you were innocent. Not only that, some prisoners were tortured to make them confess.

Governor
William Phips

On May 27, the Massachusetts Bay Colony governor William Phips set up a special court in Salem Town. The court would hear evidence, then decide if each witch suspect was guilty or innocent.

Nine important businessmen and colony leaders were chosen as trial judges. William Stoughton was the chief magistrate. The other judges included John Hathorne, Jonathan Corwin, Samuel Sewall, and Nathaniel Saltonstall.

Here's what happened if you were accused of witchcraft in Salem in 1692:

1. You were arrested.

2. A judge questioned you. If he thought you seemed guilty, you went to jail for a while.

3. You were questioned again before a group of people called a Grand Jury. They decided if you should be put on trial.

4. In the trial, judges asked questions and evidence was given. A jury decided your guilt or innocence.

5. If convicted, you were sentenced to be hanged on a certain day.

6. The sheriff carried out your death sentence.

The first witch suspect to go on trial was fifty-year-old Bridget Bishop on June 2. She had been tried for witchcraft twelve years before but had been found innocent. Still, people didn't like the flashy way she dressed and thought she was rude. She even had loud fights with her husband on Sundays! It didn't help her reputation when the trial court got her confused with a different woman named Sarah Bishop, who ran a rowdy inn where people gambled.

Just as in the earlier questioning of Sarah Good, the judges treated Bridget Bishop like she

was guilty right away. When she declared she was not a witch, the judge asked, "How can you know you are no witch, and yet not know what a witch is?"

One man told the judges that Bridget had sent her specter to him at night to sit on his chest so he could not breathe. Another said she'd made coins vanish from his pocket. The girl accusers tumbled to the floor if Bridget happened to look their way, as if her invisible specter had knocked them down.

Judge Stoughton said that if invisible specters seemed to be attacking the girl accusers during the trial, that was good enough evidence. It didn't matter that the jury couldn't see what hurt the girls, or if some appeared to be faking. Of course, this wasn't fair at all!

In Salem back then, it was up to suspects to prove they were not guilty. In courts today, it's the opposite. Now, suspects in a crime are considered innocent until they are proven guilty. They are allowed to have lawyers. If they can't afford to pay one, the court provides a lawyer. But the suspects in the witch trials were not allowed to have lawyers. They had to defend themselves. They could ask the girl accusers questions. Still, there was really no way they could prove their innocence against invisible evidence.

The jury ruled against Bridget Bishop. She was the first person to be convicted as a witch in the Salem witch trials. The punishment was as expected. She would be put to death. One judge, Nathaniel Saltonstall, didn't believe the silly evidence against her was true. He was so disgusted when other judges believed it that he quit the court.

Nathaniel Saltonstall

Witchfinders

Before Salem, there had been plenty of witch hunts in Europe. In 1486, a book called *The Hammer of Witches* was written in Germany to explain how to find and destroy witches. From the 1400s to the 1600s, over thirty thousand Europeans were accused of witchcraft. Even telling fortunes could get you in

trouble. Fearful town leaders in England sometimes paid witchfinders to start witch hunts. Witchfinders were people who had supposedly made deals with the Devil, but then had been cured. They claimed to know how the Devil's magic worked, and promised they could protect people from it. In Europe, those convicted of witchcraft were often killed in an especially horrible way. They were chained to a post, with wood piled around their feet. The wood was set on fire. The so-called witches were burned alive. There are rumors that this happened in Salem, too. But that's not true. No one convicted of witchcraft in the Salem trials was ever burned.

CHAPTER 7
Punishment

On June 10, Bridget Bishop rode in a cart from the Salem jail to Gallows Hill. A crowd of people gathered to watch. A gallows is a tall wooden frame with a rope tied to a top crossbeam. However, on this day, the rope was probably tied to the sturdy branch of a large oak tree.

Bridget Bishop was told to climb a tall ladder leaning against the tree. Then her hands were tied together and so were her feet. At the end of the rope was a big loop, called a noose. When the noose was put around her neck, her feet were pushed off the ladder so they dangled in midair. The noose slowly choked her to death. It was an extremely cruel way to die. To the very end, she kept protesting that she was not a witch.

Five days later, a group of ministers wrote to the witch-trial judges. One of the ministers was famous—Cotton Mather. He didn't scold the judges, but he did question whether spectral evidence was fair. What if the specters hurting the girls were the Devil himself, not the witch suspects at all? he asked. As everyone believed, the Devil could make himself look like any person. Cotton Mather also urged the judges to keep the courtroom calm in the future.

The judges ignored the suggestions. The court continued convicting suspects with only spectral evidence as proof. And if the girl accusers had wild, loud fits in court, they got to stay, anyway.

Cotton Mather (1663–1728)

Cotton Mather was a Puritan minister in the Massachusetts Bay Colony. He had been the youngest person ever to graduate from Harvard College at age fifteen. When he was twenty-two, he began preaching at the Old North Church with his father, Increase Mather. Cotton's beliefs about how people should live could be strict and harsh. He was gung ho about the Salem witch trials and never admitted publicly that he'd made mistakes. Later, he did something great. He championed a vaccine that prevented smallpox.

For two weeks after that first hanging, no one else was sent to jail. Then a young relative of Ann Putnam's fell ill. The Putnam family servant, Mercy Lewis, accused Rebecca Nurse and Martha Carrier of bewitching the boy. Ann Putnam and her mother had accused Rebecca Nurse of bewitching them, too, back in March. And Abigail Williams had claimed that Rebecca Nurse's specter had tried to force her to sign the Devil's book.

Rebecca Nurse

This sounded ridiculous to many people. Rebecca Nurse was a beloved, admired grandmother. She seemed like the last person to be a witch. Nevertheless, Rebecca Nurse had been questioned. Talking about the girls in court, she said, "The Lord knows I have not hurt them. I am an innocent person."

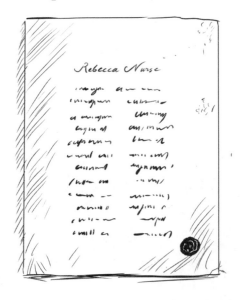

Thirty-nine people signed a statement in support of her. They all said they had known her a long time. She was a good person. No one had ever seen her practice witchcraft. Some of them offered to speak up for her in court.

All the good things said about Rebecca Nurse seemed to work. When she went on trial June 29, she was judged not guilty. But then there was an outcry from the girl accusers. So the jury voted again. The verdict this time? Guilty. Rebecca Nurse was convicted of being a witch.

On July 19, five more were executed in Salem, including Rebecca Nurse and Sarah Good. Sarah told one of the judges that if they hanged her, he would wind up drinking blood one day. Legend has it that he died of bleeding in his throat twenty-five years later.

John Proctor wrote a letter from jail asking for the Salem judges to be replaced or to have the trials moved to Boston. It didn't help him. He and four others were convicted of witchcraft. They were taken to be hanged on August 19. His wife, Elizabeth, had been found guilty, but her execution was delayed because she was pregnant.

However, George Burroughs wasn't so lucky. He died along with John Proctor that day. Before Burroughs was hanged, he said the Lord's Prayer perfectly by heart. The crowd, who had mostly believed in his guilt, suddenly wasn't so sure. Cotton Mather had once said that anyone who could recite the prayer perfectly could not be a witch. However, Mather had come to watch the hanging. He said the Devil must've helped George say the prayer. The hangings went on as planned.

When Martha Corey had been accused of witchcraft and sent to jail back in March, her husband, eighty-year-old Giles, spoke out against her. But soon, he changed his mind and said she wasn't a witch. Next thing you know, Giles Corey was accused of witchcraft, too. On September 9, he stood on trial before the judges. But there was a problem. He refused to say if he was guilty or innocent. No one had done this before. It meant the court could not move forward with his trial. Giles was stubborn, but the judges were determined to make him give an answer.

What they decided to do to him was called "pressing." It was a slow torture. While Giles was forced to lie on his back in a field near the jail, heavy stones were set on his chest. One by one, more and more were added. Officials kept asking him to say if he was guilty or not. He kept refusing. After two days of pressing, the weight of the stones crushed Giles Corey to death. This horrible death greatly upset people. Many had already started to question the fairness of the witch trials.

On September 22, eight more people who'd been convicted of witchcraft were hanged. There had been so many executions by now. Doubts troubled the villagers. Were all the deaths necessary, they wondered? What if some of the people executed—people who had been friends and neighbors—had really been innocent? Had they died for nothing?

Many in Salem and surrounding areas began speaking out against the court. At the end of October 1692, the witch trial court was closed. A new court tried the fifty-two remaining cases. But now invisible spectral evidence was no longer allowed as proof that someone was a witch. The people of New England were fed up. They'd mostly decided that this had all been a mistake. They still believed in witches, but things had spun out of control.

By May 1693, all of those in jail for witchcraft had been pardoned— even those who'd confessed or had been convicted. No more people would be hanged.

CHAPTER 8
Fortune-Telling

Five years after the trials, a minister named John Hale wrote about two Salem girls he'd met, who had dabbled in folk magic in 1692. He didn't name the girls. But according to him, they had used a well-known trick to try to tell their fortunes. They'd wanted a hint about whom they might someday marry. Girls couldn't get good jobs like men in those days. If they wanted to start their own households when they grew up, they had to get married. A lot depended on how successful their husbands turned out to be.

Hale said the girls filled a cup with water. Then they dropped the clear part of a raw egg into the water and watched it swirl. Were shapes forming? A shoe shape meant marriage to a shoemaker. A ship shape meant marriage to a sailor. However, what they saw in the cup scared them silly. A coffin shape. This was bad news. A sign of death. The girls must have been terrified and upset!

Had Hale been writing about Betty Parris and Abigail Williams? For a while, some historians believed it must be them. They thought Tituba might have shown Betty and Abigail how to practice this kind of fortune-telling. However, settlers in New England commonly used everyday household objects like this to try to tell their

John Hale

future or bring luck. And there are no records that show Tituba practiced black magic on her own.

Reverend Hale wrote, "I fear that some young persons through a vain curiosity to know their future condition, have tampered with the Devil's tools so far that hereby the door was open to Satan to play those pranks . . . (in) . . . 1692." He also wrote that he had healed one of the girls and ended her bewitchment, saying, "She was speedily released from the bonds of Satan." Did he mean Betty? Near the end of March 1692, her parents sent her from the village to stay with relatives in Salem Town. They'd hoped she'd have a chance at getting well if she wasn't involved in the trials. She did seem to recover after a while.

And what about Abigail? Hale wrote that the other girl who was trying to see her fortune that day never got married. He said she was haunted for the rest of her life because she had tried fortune-telling. This should be a warning to others not to try it, he claimed. No one knows what really happened to Abigail, though.

If Betty and Abigail were the girls in Hale's story, they might have felt guilty afterward for doing something as forbidden as fortune-telling. Did they worry they were bad girls? Even evil girls? Mr. Parris was a stern, strict Puritan. They might have been afraid to tell him what they had done. Maybe they began acting strangely in January

1692 as a way to get someone to notice them and help them get over their fears.

It's also likely the two girls had heard about the strange case of the Goodwin children in Boston. The children had claimed a witch was hurting them. They'd begun having fits. The Parris family had lived in Boston while this was going on. Later, in Salem, Betty and Abigail may have simply copied the Goodwin children's behavior.

Reverend Parris

However, no one else ever confirmed the story Hale told. The identity of the two girls he wrote about remains a mystery.

It's also possible that Betty and Abigail weren't faking their fits. They might have truly been sick, but in a way that had nothing to do with witches. They may have gotten food poisoning. Puritans made bread with rye grain. Rye could go bad from a plant fungus called ergot. Ergot grew best after cold winters followed by rainy springs. That was just the kind of weather Salem had in 1692. If the girls ate poisoned rye, it could have caused them to see things that weren't really there. Their bodies might twitch and jerk.

However, ergot can be deadly, and none of the Salem girls died. Also, some of the girls' fits seemed to start and stop when they wanted them to. About seventy-four people (mostly in the Massachusetts Bay Colony) accused others of witchcraft during the Salem scare. If any of these accusers' fits were real, not faked, the girls most likely to have been sick were probably Betty and Abigail.

CHAPTER 9
Why?

Someone was assigned to write down everything that was said every day of the Salem witch trials. Still, it's hard to know the truth today. Court officials, accusers, witnesses, and suspects all spoke quickly. If people talked at the same time or mumbled, it was hard to hear. Accusers might have fits that were hard to describe. It was up to the writer to figure out and record everyone's words

and actions. So their notes aren't totally accurate and can be misunderstood.

Many people think most or all of the girls were faking. Some of them might have gotten so caught up in their made-up accusations that they halfway believed them themselves. Or maybe once they had told so many lies and caused the deaths of innocent people, they decided there was no going back. They feared punishment if they told the truth.

It sounds coldhearted, but some of the girl accusers may have thought this was all a game. Girls in the colonies worked hard. They might cook at the hearth fire, wash clothes in boiling pots, sweep

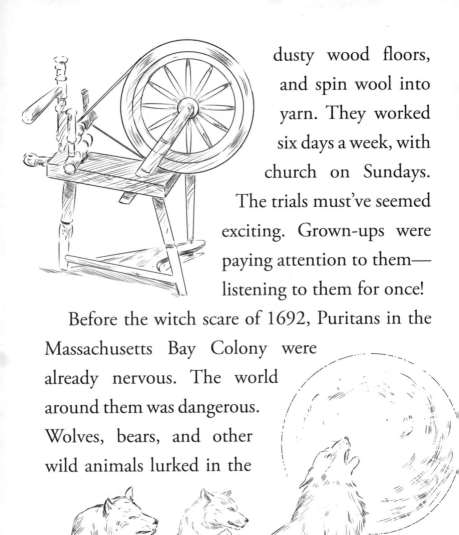

dusty wood floors, and spin wool into yarn. They worked six days a week, with church on Sundays. The trials must've seemed exciting. Grown-ups were paying attention to them—listening to them for once!

Before the witch scare of 1692, Puritans in the Massachusetts Bay Colony were already nervous. The world around them was dangerous. Wolves, bears, and other wild animals lurked in the

nearby forest. They could snatch a child or kill the family cow at any minute. And English and French soldiers were fighting in the colonies. Native Americans sided with the French and attacked settlers in Maine and Canada. People in Salem worried they might be next.

Not only that, there was also trouble between the farmers in Salem Village and merchants in Salem Town. The villagers stuck to strict church teachings.

Over in town, things were changing. Villagers worried that evil could creep into their lives if they and their neighbors strayed from God.

When a group of people begin feeling fearful like this, they may look for a scapegoat. A scapegoat is someone to blame for your troubles. Maybe the Puritans thought that if they punished the witch suspects, everything would get back to normal and they'd feel safe. Of course, that didn't happen.

During the Salem witch trials, about two hundred people were unfairly accused of witchcraft. Over fifty of them confessed. Five died in jail, including Sarah Osborne and Sarah Good's baby. Dorcas, Sarah Good's other child, spent eight months in jail and became mentally ill. Twenty innocent people (fourteen women and six men) were executed, nineteen by hanging and one by pressing. It was a terrible tragedy.

Halloween

Today Halloween is simply a fun holiday that is about dressing up in costumes and getting candy. It began long ago as a harvest celebration at the end of October, mainly in Ireland and Scotland. There were bonfires and jack-o'-lanterns carved from turnips and other vegetables. During this time, people thought the imaginary wall between the world of the dead and the real world became extra thin. Evil spirits could enter the real world more easily. People believed it was easier for the Devil to bewitch others then, especially women. Over the years, this idea turned into a belief that women could become witches. There are no real broom-flying evil witches like the one in *The Wizard of Oz* movie. Those are only found in fiction.

CHAPTER 10
Afterward

After the witch trials, many people felt sorry or guilty about taking part in them. Others didn't. Judge Stoughton did not feel guilty. However, Judge Sewall publicly apologized. So did all twelve people on the trial jury.

In January 1697, the Massachusetts Bay Colony held an official day of prayer and fasting to ask forgiveness for wrongdoings, especially in the trials. Some people just wanted to forget the trials' tragic events. They wanted everyone to forget. So they may have destroyed papers and evidence.

In 1694, Reverend Parris asked those gathered in the Salem church to forgive him for encouraging the trials. He said, "Through weakness, ignorance, etc., I may have been mistaken." He hoped that "we may forgive each other heartily." He was probably really sorry, but he was also trying to keep his job. Many in Salem had grown to dislike him by now. They wanted him to quit. In 1697, he did.

A new minister named Joseph Green took over Salem Village church. He was good at solving problems. He rearranged seating in the church so that people who didn't get along had to sit beside each other and talk. Slowly things began to calm down. Still, no one could really forget.

Joseph Green

Twelve-year-old Ann Putnam had accused as many as sixty-two people during the witch hunt. Her parents died seven years after the trials, when she was nineteen. She had to begin taking care of all nine of her younger brothers and sisters. In 1706, she wrote an apology that was read aloud by Reverend Green in the church. In the apology she said she had been "made an instrument for the accusing of several persons of a grievous crime, whereby their lives were taken away from them."

Ann went on to say that she now had "good reason to believe they were innocent." Did she mean that someone had forced her to accuse others of witchcraft? If so, was it someone in her family? Or another girl? We'll probably never know. Ann did not marry, and died at age thirty-six.

Her cousin, Mary Walcott, accused more people of witchcraft than anyone else. Sixty-nine!

Abigail Williams had testified in court for the last time on June 3, 1692. This seems odd since the trials continued for nearly eight more months. There is no record of what happened to her after that. It was as if she disappeared.

Abigail had accused forty-one people of witchcraft. How many did her cousin Betty Parris accuse? Three—Tituba, Sarah Good, and Sarah Osborne. Betty never came to speak in any trial after she left the village in March. When she was twenty-seven, she married a shoemaker named Benjamin Baron. They had four children. No one knows

how she felt about her part in what happened.

Mercy Lewis wasn't about to apologize for anything she'd done. She kept on accusing people of being witches all the way into 1693.

Tituba was in jail for over a year. She said that Reverend Parris promised to pay all of her jail fees. He never did. She was finally sold and became the slave of a new owner in May 1693. No one knows where she or her husband, John, went after that.

In the end, Elizabeth Proctor and her newborn baby were released from jail along with the rest of those who'd been accused or convicted of witchcraft. However, her troubles weren't over. Like others, she'd lost her wealth, health, and good reputation. Some people were even worse off than she was. Instead of going free, they had to remain in jail because they couldn't pay the fees for the time they had already been held there!

The House of the Seven Gables

There is a famous house in Salem today that stood there during the witch trials. It's nicknamed the House of the Seven Gables after a book published in 1851 by Nathaniel Hawthorne. His great-great-grandfather was John Hathorne, one of the judges in the Salem witch trials. When Nathaniel visited a cousin who lived in the house, he got the idea to write a story. It would be about a fictional family who owned the house. In his book, a character named Colonel Pyncheon accuses an innocent man of witchcraft during the Salem trials in 1692. After the man is hanged, the colonel steals the man's land and builds the house on it. But because of the unjust thing he'd done, the colonel's family is cursed for the next 150 years. You can visit the real house in Salem that he wrote about. It has a secret passage and seven gables, just like in the book. A gable is the triangle shape on a house that's formed where two slanted roofs meet.

Nathaniel
Hawthorne

In Salem, you can visit Gallows Hill and sites such as the Salem Witch Museum and Rebecca Nurse's homestead. The burial places of the twenty executed for witchcraft are unknown. They're not in the main cemetery. Convicted witches couldn't be buried there. Families may have claimed their relatives' bodies on Gallows Hill and buried them privately. Others were probably buried right where they were hanged.

You can also go to the Salem Witch Trials Memorial. It was built in Salem in 1992, three hundred years after the trials. It is meant to honor those who died so needlessly and tragically in 1692. The memorial is a long stone wall with twenty stone benches jutting out along it. There's one bench for each person executed in the trials. His or her name is inscribed on it, as well as how and when the deaths occurred. Words they spoke during their trials are carved on other stones along the wall as well.

IN MEMORY OF THOSE INNOCENTS
WHO DIED DURING THE
SALEM VILLAGE WITCHCRAFT HYSTERIA
OF 1692

In 1711 and 1957, many people found guilty of witchcraft during the Salem witch trials were cleared of any wrongdoing. On Halloween, October 31, 2001, the governor of Massachusetts cleared the remaining ones. At last, all of those who'd been jailed or convicted as witches in 1692 were officially declared innocent.

Timeline of the Salem Witch Trials

1689	— Cotton Mather publishes his book about the Goodwin witchcraft case in Boston
	— Samuel Parris becomes the church minister in Salem Village
1692:	
January	— Betty Parris and Abigail Williams begin having fits
February 24	— A doctor says the girls are bewitched
February 25	— Tituba and John Indian bake a witch cake
February 27	— Ann Putnam and Elizabeth Hubbard begin having fits
March 1	— The first suspects are questioned
May 27	— Salem's witch trial court is formed
June 10	— Bridget Bishop is hanged for witchcraft
July 19	— Sarah Good, Elizabeth Howe, Susannah Martin, Rebecca Nurse and Sarah Wildes are hanged as witches
August 19	— George Burroughs, Martha Carrier, George Jacobs, John Proctor, and John Willard are hanged as witches
September 19	— Giles Corey is pressed and dies two days later
September 22	— Martha Corey, Mary Easty, Alice Parker, Mary Parker, Ann Pudeator, Wilmot Redd, Margaret Scott, and Samuel Wardwell are hanged as witches
October 29	— The Salem witch trial court closes
1693	— In May, everyone in jail for witchcraft is freed
1706	— Ann Putnam apologizes for taking part in the witchcraft trial
2001	— Massachusetts officially proclaims that all those convicted in the Salem witchcraft trials of 1692 were innocent

Timeline of the World

1620	The Pilgrims arrive on the *Mayflower* to begin Plymouth Colony in Massachusetts
1630	Puritans settle Massachusetts Bay Colony near Boston
1633	The astronomer Galileo goes on trial in Rome for saying the sun is at the center of the universe
1642	Dutch artist Rembrandt van Rijn paints *Night Watch*
1644	The Ming Dynasty ends in China
1653	The Taj Mahal is completed in India
1661	Louis XIV begins building a palace in Versailles, France
1665	The Great Plague in London kills 70,000 people
1666	The Great Fire of London burns 13,000 houses
1667	John Milton finishes his epic poem, *Paradise Lost*
1669	Mount Etna erupts
1682	William Penn founds the Commonwealth of Pennsylvania
	Peter the Great becomes Tsar of Russia
1690	First recorded sighting of the planet Uranus
1691	Plymouth Colony becomes part of Massachusetts Bay Colony
1694	The Bank of England is created
	Three hundred and twenty slaves die on the English ship *Hannibal*'s voyage from Africa to North America

Bibliography

* **Books for young readers**

*Aronson, Marc. *Witch-Hunt: Mysteries of the Salem Witch Trials.* New York: Simon & Schuster, 2005.

Foulds, Diane E. *Death in Salem: The Private Lives Behind the 1692 Witch Hunt.* Guilford, CT: Globe Pequot Press, 2010.

Goss, K. David. *The Salem Witch Trials: A Reference Guide.* Westport, CT: Greenwood Press, 2008.

Hill, Frances. *A Delusion of Satan: The Full Story of the Salem Witch Trials.* Boston: Da Capo Press, 2002.

Hill, Frances. *Hunting for Witches: A Visitor's Guide to the Salem Witch Trials.* Beverly, MA: Commonwealth Editions, 2002.

*Krensky, Stephen. *Witch Hunt: It Happened in Salem Village.* New York: Random House, Inc., 1989.

Norton, Mary Beth. *In the Devil's Snare: The Salem Witchcraft Crisis of 1692.* New York: Alfred A. Knopf, 2002.

Roach, Marilynne K. *The Salem Witch Trials: A Day-By-Day Chronicle of a Community Under Seige.* Lanham, MD: Taylor Trade Publishing, 2004.

*Schanzer, Rosalyn. *Witches! The Absolutely True Tale of Disaster in Salem.* Washington, DC: National Geographic Society, 2011.

Starkey, Marion. *The Devil in Massachusetts.* New York: Doubleday, 1961.

Weisman, Richard. *Witchcraft, Magic, and Religion in 17th-century Massachusetts.* Amherst, MA: University of Massachusetts Press, 1984.

A 1494 edition of *Malleus Maleficarum* (*The Hammer of Witches*), a witchfinders' manual

Woodcut of a Puritan family, 1563

Portrait of Cotton Mather

The Wonders of the Invisible World:

Being an Account of the

TRYALS

OF

Several Witches,

Lately Excuted in

NEW-ENGLAND:

And of several remarkable Curiosities therein Occurring.

Together with,

I. Observations upon the Nature, the Number, and the Operations of the Devils.

II. A short Narrative of a late outrage committed by a knot of Witches in *Swede-Land*, very much resembling, and so far explaining, that under which *New-England* has laboured.

III. Some Councels directing a due Improvement of the Terrible things lately done by the unusual and amazing Range of *Evil-Spirits* in *New-England*.

IV. A brief Discourse upon those *Temptations* which are the more ordinary Devices of Satan.

By COTTON MATHER.

Published by the Special Command of his EXCELLENCY the Govencur of the Province of the *Massachusetts-Bay* in *New-England*.

Printed first, at *Boston* in *New-England*; and Reprinted at *London*, for *John Dunton*, at the *Raven* in the *Poultry*. 1693.

Title page of Cotton Mather's book on witchcraft

An engraving of Puritans going to church

Nineteenth-century print of the courtroom erupting

The girls "see" a flock of yellow birds

A reconstruction of the Salem Village meetinghouse

Ergot grows on rye

The Burying Point in Salem, Massachusetts

The Witch House is the only building in Salem that dates back to the witch trials

The House of the Seven Gables

Salem, Massachusetts, today

The Witch Trials Memorial

The Salem Maritime National Historic Site

A scene from Arthur Miller's play *The Crucible*